I Love Cats and Kittens

David Alderton

SCHOLASTIC

❧ SCHOLASTIC

This edition published by Scholastic Inc., 557 Broadway, New York, NY 10012, by arrangement with QEB Publishing, Inc.

Scholastic and associated logos are trademarks and/or registered trademarks of Scholastic Inc.

Distributed by
Scholastic Canada. Ltd., Markham, Ontario
Scholastic New Zealand Ltd., Greenmount, Auckland
Scholastic Australia Pty. Ltd., Gosford NSW
Scholastic UK, Warwickshire Coventry

Editor: Tasha Percy
In-house Designer: Krina Patel
Art Director: Laura Roberts-Jensen
Designer: Melissa Alaverdy

Copyright © QEB Publishing, Inc. 2014

A CIP record for this book is available from the Library of Congress.

ISBN: 978-0-545-72224-7

10 9 8 7 6 5 4 3 2 1 0

Printed in Shenzhen City, China

Contents

Abyssinian

The founding cat of this breed was brought back from the East African country of Abyssinia, which is now known as Ethiopia. Abyssinians have a special type of tabby markings. This makes their coat look sparkly. They are very friendly cats that enjoy playing.

American Bobtail

The American Bobtail has a much shorter tail than most cats, measuring between a half and a third of their length. This breed is often shorthaired, with tabby markings. All of today's American Bobtails are related to an abandoned kitten found in the state of Arizona.

American Curl

The curly ears of these cats are really unusual! There is a choice of short and longer coated American Curls, both of which have slim bodies. These cats are descended from a stray that moved in with a California couple in 1981.

American Shorthair

Descended from street cats, the American Shorthair can be seen at many cat shows. It is a strong, muscular cat, bred in a wide range of colors and patterns. American Shorthairs with tabby markings are most common. They are friendly cats by nature.

American Wirehair

Here is a cat whose coat feels very different, with an unusual wiry feel. The hairs, including the whiskers, may be curly. The first American Wirehair cat was bred on a farm in upstate New York, and even today, these cats are rare. Their unusual coat needs no special care.

Angora

Active and lively, the Angora has been developed from crossings of Abyssinian and Siamese cats. Angoras have long bodies with soft, silky coats. Their fur is longer on the body than the face and does not mat, or tangle easily. Angoras enjoy chasing after toys.

Australian Mist

The first cats of this breed were spotted, but now there are others with marbled patterning. The markings on the coat of the Australian Mist are not that clear. They appear misty, and that's how they got their name. These are gentle cats, and tend not to scratch, nor do they like hunting.

Balinese

These elegant cats are the longhaired form of the Siamese breed, and they have similar patterning with stunning blue eyes. They have a thin coat, and this helps to emphasize their athletic body. Balinese like climbing and jumping.

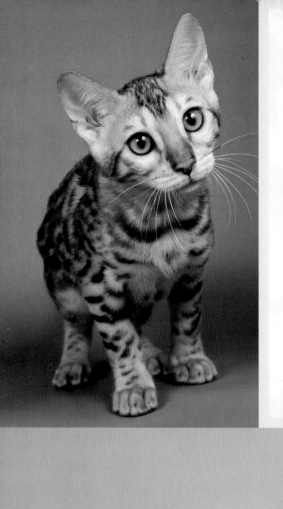

Bengal

This breed is the result of matings between wild Asian Leopard Cats and domestic cats. This explains why Bengals often keep their tail close to the ground when walking, like wild cats. They love climbing and are often fascinated with water, too. They enjoy trying to catch the drops from a dripping tap.

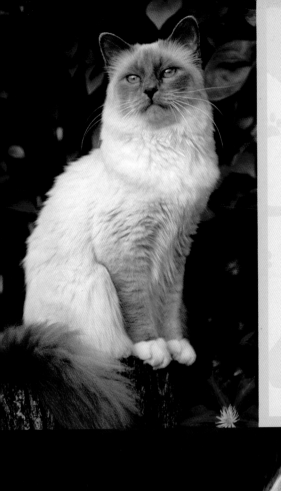

Birman

There is no mistaking a Birman, because of its unusual markings. It has white areas on its front feet, known as gloves. White fur also extends up the back of the legs, and these markings are called boots. Whatever their actual coat color, Birmans always have blue eyes.

Bombay

Looking just like a miniature black panther, the Bombay has jet black, glossy fur. Its eyes are usually coppery in color, but sometimes green. These are easy cats to look after, but may be greedy, putting on weight. Bombays are happy living with dogs.

25

British Longhair

These cats are the longhaired form of the British Shorthair, and so their coats will need more grooming and care. British Longhairs are bred in a wide range of colors and patterns to their short-coated cousins and have the same laid-back personality.

British Shorthair

This breed was developed from ordinary street cats, and over time, new colors were created. Almost every color and pattern that you can think of in cats can now be seen in this breed. British Shorthairs have become much larger than ordinary pet cats. They are intelligent, friendly, and playful.

Burmese

As a result of differences in their ancestry, Burmese in North America now have more rounded faces than those seen in Europe. You can choose Burmese in a range of colors; their eyes normally vary from yellowish to gold. They are good as indoor cats and play well with dogs and children.

Burmilla

Bred for its friendly nature as much as its beautiful coloring, the Burmilla is a great choice of pet. Its coat "sparkles" as it moves. Its name reflects the two breeds from which it was bred in 1981. These were the Burmese and the Chinchilla Longhair.

California Spangled

The aim of Paul Casey, who created this unusual breed, was to develop a domestic cat with a spotted coat that looked and walked like a small leopard. He hoped it would remind people of how the wild relatives of domestic cats were becoming threatened.

Chartreux

The grayish fur—known as blue in the cat world—is a main feature of the ancient Chartreux breed. In fact, this is the only color these cats come in. They are Europe's oldest cat breed, whose descendants have lived at the same monastery in France for more than 800 years.

Chausie

These cats are bigger than ordinary domestic cats. This is because they are descended partly from the jungle cat, a wild species that played a part in their early breeding. Chausies can jump the height of a person, run along tree branches, and are very active cats.

39

Cornish Rex

A litter of farm cats born during the 1950s in the county of Cornwall, southwestern England, included a kitten with an unusually short, curly coat. He was named Kallibunker and became the founder of the Cornish Rex breed. These cats can sit up on their hind legs just like dogs.

Cymric

This is the longhaired form of the Manx cat, and as a result, some Cymrics have no trace of a tail. The Cymric has an easygoing, playful nature, and will live happily in a home with a dog. It has a reputation for having a long lifespan.

Devon Rex

These elf-like cats are mischievous in nature, and love playing games, such as chasing after balls. They soon learn to recognize the sound of their names and come when called. Their soft, thin coat does not protect them well from the cold. They do not enjoy going outdoors in bad weather.

Egyptian Mau

Egypt in the Middle East is where cats became popular pets thousands of years ago. This breed is descended from the street cats and has a spotted tabby pattern. The word *"mau"* means "cat" in Egyptian, and probably comes from the "meow" sound that cats make.

European Shorthair

Bred from the street cats of Europe, the European Shorthair is hardy and friendly by nature and adaptable, too. Their short coats need little grooming, and they can be seen in many colors and patterns. European Shorthairs usually live happily alongside dogs that share their home.

Exotic Shorthair

Looking like a teddy bear with its flat face, big round eyes, and cuddly coat, the Exotic is the result of breeding between Persian Longhairs and American Shorthairs. It has now become very popular, especially in North America and can be seen in a wide range of colors and patterns.

Havana Brown

This cat is an attractive warm, chocolate-brown shade. Its eyes are always green and oval in shape. Lively and playful, the Havana Brown is a relative of the Siamese and has a similar athletic build.

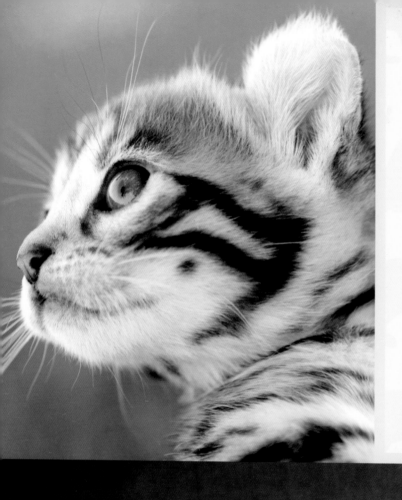

Highlander

This breed is very easy to recognize because it has slightly curled ears combined with a short bobtail. Highlanders exist in almost any color or pattern, and they can have long or short fur. They love to play and have lots of energy!

55

Japanese Bobtail

These cats are often black and white, or tortoiseshell and white, although they are bred in other colors, too. They have unusual pompom tails. Their habit of sitting in windows with a raised paw inspired the Japanese tradition of placing a ceramic ornament called "*Maneki Neko*"—meaning the "Beckoning Cat"—in windows to greet visitors.

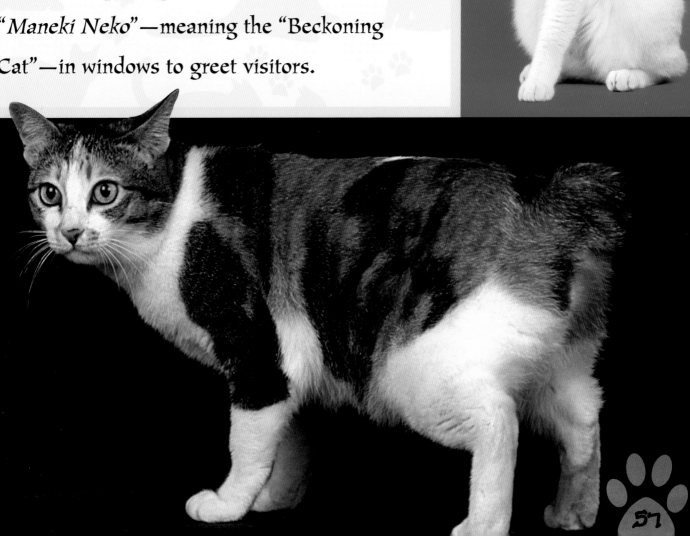

Korat

This ancient breed comes from the northeastern province of Korat, Thailand. The Korat has a distinctive silvery-blue coat. Young cats have yellowish eyes that later change to a beautiful shade of green. These cats were traditionally given in pairs as wedding gifts to wish couples good luck.

Kurilian Bobtail

The homeland of these rare cats is the Kuril Islands, near Russia and Japan. It is thought that they are descended from cats taken there by sailors from mainland Asia many centuries ago. They have a large head, tabby patterning, and a short bobtail.

Lambkin

With fur that can look like lamb's wool, this breed has the coat of a Selkirk Rex combined with the short legs of a Munchkin. These cats can climb very well, both in the home and outside in the garden and are affectionate by nature.

LaPerm

All of today's LaPerms trace their ancestry back to a farm cat born in 1982 on a fruit farm in Oregon. These cats have loose, bouncy fur, with longhaired members of this breed having bigger coats. LaPerm kittens are often bald at birth, and their fur grows slowly.

Maine Coon

This was the first breed developed in the U.S., in the state of Maine. During the 1800s, these cats were commonly kept on farms. Today, the Maine Coon has become the most popular cat breed in the world. Males grow larger than females.

Manx

Hundreds of years ago, cats on the Isle of Man, off England's northwestern coast, started to give birth to kittens without tails. The Manx are bred in many colors, often having white areas in their coats. These cats are playful and intelligent by nature. Manx have been featured on the island's coins and stamps.

Munchkin

These cats are a new breed and can be easily recognized by their short legs. There are both short and long-coated forms. People used to worry that the short legs would handicap these cats, but this has not proved to be a problem. They run fast, although they cannot jump far.

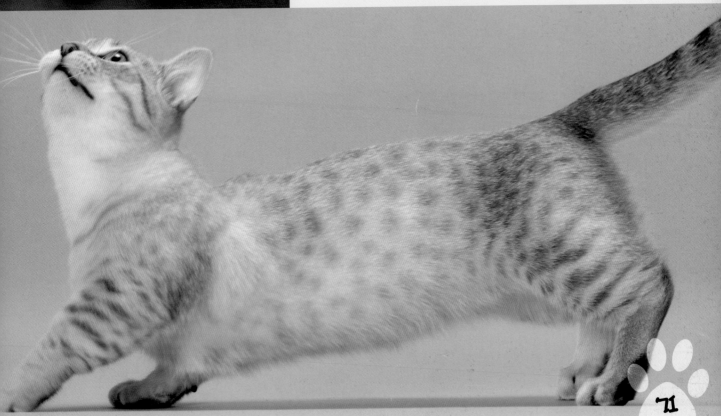

Nebelung

Kittens of this breed are born with blue eyes, but they change to green or sometimes yellowish-green. The distinctive blue-gray coat of a Nebelung has a silky texture and is of medium length. They are related to the Russian breed and are currently rare.

73

Norwegian Forest Cat

Bred to survive in the bitterly cold winters of Norway, these are large cats with dense, water-repellent coats. They shed their thick fur in the spring, losing their ruff— the area of long fur under the chin. Tabbies are common. These cats like to roam outside.

75

Ocicat

The stunning appearance of wild cats has often attracted breeders who want to create domestic cats with similar patterning. In this case, a breed was developed that displayed the spotted markings of the Ocelot, which lives in parts of Central and South America.

Oriental

These cats exist in more colors and patterns than any other breed. There are hundreds of possible varieties. Orientals are playful, active, and vocal cats with large ears and an elegant body shape.

Persian

This cat dates back to the late 1800s and was one of the first recognized purebreds. Aside from their long coats, which require a lot of grooming to prevent the hair from becoming matted, Persians have short noses and small ears, too. They exist in many different colors and patterns.

Peterbald

This relatively new breed was created in St. Petersburg, Russia, in 1993. The coat length of these cats varies widely. The whiskers can be curly in some cases, too. In terms of body shape, the Peterbald looks like a Siamese cat.

Pixiebob

This unusual breed resembles a miniature Bobcat, as reflected by its very short tail and build. Pixiebobs are often brown tabbies. They may look like wild cats, but DNA tests have shown that they are simply domestic cats.

Ragamuffin

Ragamuffins are large cats that have been carefully bred to ensure they are gentle by nature, just like their ancestor, the Ragdoll. They have been created in a wide range of colors and patterns. Their long coats do not mat easily and are very soft.

87

Ragdoll

The name of these cats comes from the way that they relax when they are picked up, lying in your arms like a rag doll. They are also one of the few breeds that display little, if any, hunting instincts, meaning that they will not harm wildlife.

Russian

In the 1860s these cats were developed around the Port of Archangel, in the far north of Russia, and from there they were taken to England and other European countries. They were known for a time both as the Archangel and Russian Blue, but other colors such as white now exist, too.

Savannah

Named after the plains of Africa, these cats are hybrids—being the result of matings between the wild Serval and domestic cats. They are the largest breed, much bigger than ordinary cats, and have spotted patterning. They may greet people by bouncing up to them, like a dog!

Scottish Fold

The cute appearance of these cats stems not just from the way their ears are folded down, but also the rounded shape of their face. The first Scottish Fold kitten, called Susie, cropped up on a farm in Scotland in 1961. There are now long and short-haired forms of these affectionate cats.

96

Selkirk Rex

Descended from an abandoned kitten brought into a rescue shelter in Montana, this breed is named after the nearby Selkirk Mountains. It is a typical Rex breed, with a curly coat, and exists in both short and long-coated varieties. They are large cats with round faces.

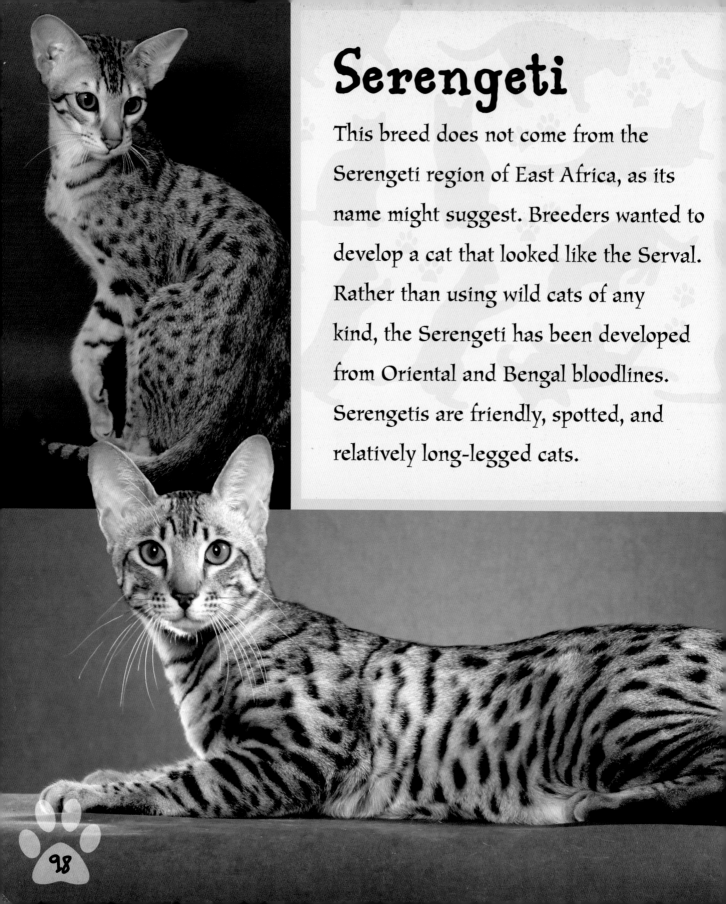

Serengeti

This breed does not come from the Serengeti region of East Africa, as its name might suggest. Breeders wanted to develop a cat that looked like the Serval. Rather than using wild cats of any kind, the Serengeti has been developed from Oriental and Bengal bloodlines. Serengetis are friendly, spotted, and relatively long-legged cats.

Siamese

Sleek, short-coated, and noisy, the Siamese is one of the best-known breeds. Kittens are born white, and only develop the darker areas of coloration on their legs, feet, face, ears, and tail over time. These areas of the body are described as the points.

Siberian

Well-protected against the freezing cold of the Siberian winter, these cats roamed the countryside for hundreds of years before they came to the attention of cat breeders. As with many longhaired cats, their coat becomes thicker and longer during the winter, and then is shed in the spring.

Singapura

The ancestors of this breed were discovered living wild in the Asian country of Singapore. They became known locally as "drain cats", because they used to shelter in storm drains. The Singapura is a ticked tabby. This means Singapuras have alternating dark brown and ivory-white banding running down their hairs. They are also one of the smallest breeds of cat.

Snowshoe

White markings on the front feet help to identify the Snowshoe. A white stripe is present, extending between the eyes and broadening over the nose and around the jaws. This is known as a blaze. The eyes are blue, reflecting the part played by the Siamese in the breed's ancestry.

Sokoke

This breed is named after the Sokoke forest region in Kenya, Africa, where the ancestors of this breed were discovered in 1978. Their patterning is very distinct, as is their behavior. They often walk on tiptoe, and the male cat helps the female take care of their kittens.

Somali

Somalis are the long-coated form of the Abyssinian breed, and they are similar in nature. If you look closely at their coat, you will see alternating light and dark bands of color extending along the length of their hairs. The Somali is a cautious breed that loves to play and cuddle.

Sphynx

Although sometimes called the hairless cat, the Sphynx can have traces of hair present on its body. These cats are not only at risk from the cold, but they can suffer sunburn easily, too, particularly where there are pink areas of skin. They are generally best kept indoors.

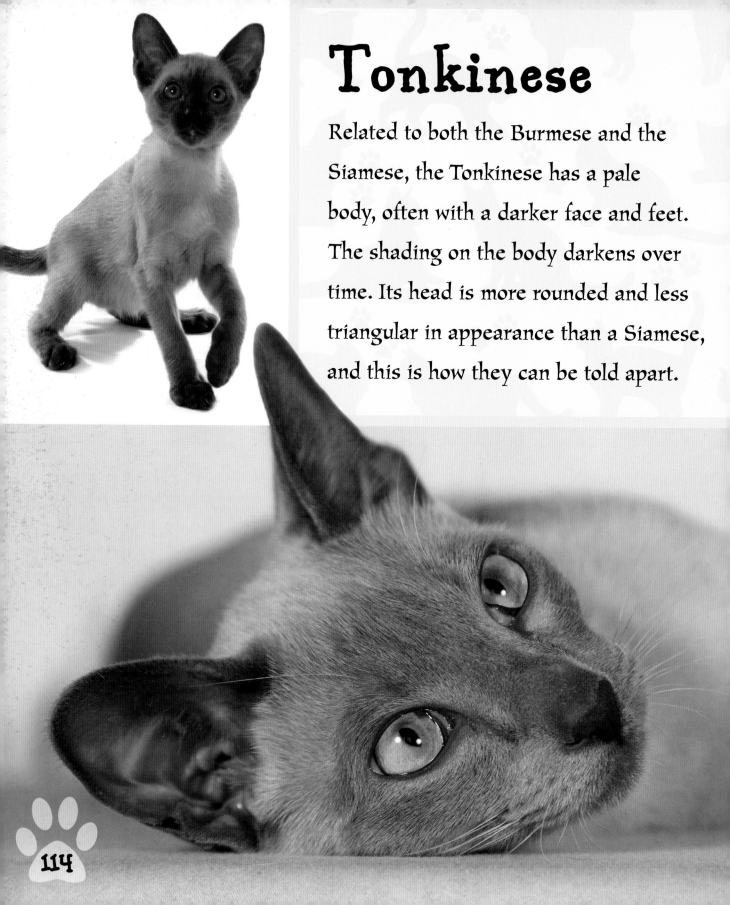

Tonkinese

Related to both the Burmese and the Siamese, the Tonkinese has a pale body, often with a darker face and feet. The shading on the body darkens over time. Its head is more rounded and less triangular in appearance than a Siamese, and this is how they can be told apart.

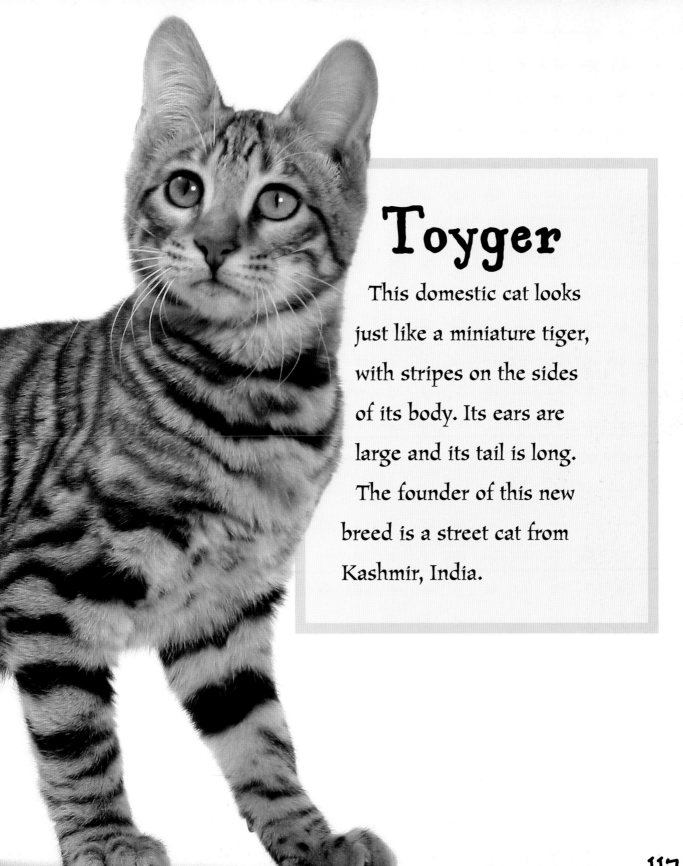

Toyger

This domestic cat looks just like a miniature tiger, with stripes on the sides of its body. Its ears are large and its tail is long. The founder of this new breed is a street cat from Kashmir, India.

Turkish Angora

These cats have been kept in the area of Angora, Turkey, for thousands of years. They are often white in color and were probably the ancestor of the Persian Longhair. Their coat has a very distinctive, silky texture, but they do not have a thick undercoat.

Turkish Van

This breed is found around Lake Van in Turkey. Although many people think cats dislike water, Turkish Van cats often go swimming in the lake in summer to cool down when it is very hot.